T0071104

Mack Wilberg
Anthems

9 anthems for mixed voices
by Mack Wilberg

MUSIC DEPARTMENT

OXFORD
UNIVERSITY PRESS

OXFORD
UNIVERSITY PRESS

Great Clarendon Street, Oxford OX2 6DP,
United Kingdom

Oxford University Press is a department of the University of Oxford.
It furthers the University's objective of excellence in research, scholarship,
and education by publishing worldwide. Oxford is a registered trade mark of
Oxford University Press in the UK and in certain other countries

© Oxford University Press 2013

Mack Wilberg has asserted his right under the Copyright, Designs
and Patents Act, 1988, to be identified as the Composer of these Works

First published 2013

Impression: 4

All rights reserved. No part of this publication may be reproduced,
stored in a retrieval system, or transmitted, in any form or by any means,
without the prior permission in writing of Oxford University Press

Permission to perform the works in this anthology in public
(except in the course of divine worship) should normally be obtained from
a local performing right licensing organization, unless the owner or the occupier
of the premises being used already holds a licence from such an organization.
Likewise, permission to make and exploit a recording of these works
should be obtained from a local mechanical copyright licensing organization

Enquiries concerning reproduction outside the scope of the above
should be directed to the Music Rights Department, Oxford University Press, at
music.permissions.uk@oup.com or at the address above

ISBN 978-0-19-339819-1

Music and text origination by
Enigma Music Production Services, Amersham Bucks.

Printed in Great Britain on acid-free paper by
Halstan & Co. Ltd, Amersham, Bucks.

Contents

Index of Orchestrations and Vocal Scores	4
Available Recordings	5
Beautiful Saviour	6
Benediction	8
Brother James's Air	14
I sing the mighty power of God (*O little town of Bethlehem*)	20
King of glory, King of peace	28
Morning has broken	38
O Light of Life!	43
O praise ye the Lord	51
The Morning Trumpet	60

Composer's note

Most of the music in this collection was written for choirs I have had the privilege of working with over the past thirty years. Included are both original works and arrangements, as well as two commissioned pieces published here for the first time.

I have made new SATB versions of several pieces originally written for men's voices and also reduced the accompaniment from piano, four-hands to organ only for one of the arrangements. With the exception of the unaccompanied pieces, all selections included in the collection may be sung with alternative orchestral accompaniment (see page 4 for details).

I would like to thank David Blackwell for his invaluable assistance in the making of this volume.

MACK WILBERG
June 2013

Index of Orchestrations and Vocal Scores

The following items are also available as listed below:

- Scores and orchestral parts on hire/rental from the publisher or appropriate agent;
- Separate vocal scores on sale.

Benediction

- Orchestration: 2fl, ob, 2cl, 4hn, harp, strings
- Vocal score for SATB and keyboard (piano or organ) on sale: 978-0-19-337223-8

Brother James's Air

- Orchestration: 2fl, 2ob, 2cl, 2bsn, 4hn, strings
- Vocal score for SATB and keyboard (piano or organ) on sale: 978-0-19-337224-5

I sing the mighty power of God

- Orchestration: picc, fl, ob, 3hn, perc, glock, harp (opt.), strings
- Vocal score for SATB and organ on sale: 978-0-19-386923-3

King of glory, King of peace

- Orchestration: 2fl, picc/fl3, 2ob, 2cl, 2bsn, 2hn, 2tpt, timp, perc, glock, harp, strings

Morning has broken

- Orchestration: 3fl, 2ob, 2cl, 2bsn, 4hn, glock, harp, strings
- Vocal score for SATB and piano four-hands on sale: 978-0-19-380463-0

O Light of Life!

- Orchestration: 3fl, 2ob, 2cl, 2bsn, 4hn, organ (opt.), strings
- Vocal score for SATB and organ (3 staves) on sale: 978-0-19-380459-3

O little town of Bethlehem

- Orchestration: picc, fl, ob, 3hn, perc (glock), harp (opt.), strings

O praise ye the Lord

- Orchestration: 3fl, 2ob, 2cl, 2bsn, 4hn, 3tpt, 3tbne, tba, timp, perc, organ, strings

The Morning Trumpet

- Vocal score for unaccompanied lower voices (TTBB) on sale: 978-0-19-386828-1

Available Recordings

Beautiful Saviour
The version for men's voices has been recorded on the CD *Men of the Mormon Tabernacle Choir* (SKU 5053126).

Benediction
The orchestral arrangement has been recorded by the Mormon Tabernacle Choir and the Orchestra at Temple Square on the CD *Heavensong: Music of Contemplation and Light* (SKU 5035926).

Brother James's Air
The orchestral arrangement has been recorded by the Mormon Tabernacle Choir and the Orchestra at Temple Square on the CD *Heavensong: Music of Contemplation and Light* (SKU 5035926).

I sing the mighty power of God
The orchestral arrangement has been recorded by the Mormon Tabernacle Choir and the Orchestra at Temple Square on the CD *Consider the Lilies* (SKU 4537795).

Morning has broken
The orchestral arrangement has been recorded by the Mormon Tabernacle Choir and the Orchestra at Temple Square on the CD *Consider the Lilies* (SKU 4537795).

O Light of Life!
The orchestral arrangement has been recorded by the Mormon Tabernacle Choir and the Orchestra at Temple Square on the CD *Mack Wilberg: Requiem and other choral works* (SKU 4996466).

The Morning Trumpet
The version for men's voices has been recorded on the CD *Men of the Mormon Tabernacle Choir* (SKU 5053126).

originally written for the Brigham Young University Men's Chorus

Beautiful Saviour

Anon., 12th century

Silesian Folk Melody
arr. MACK WILBERG

© Oxford University Press 2013. This collection © Oxford University Press 2013.

25
fair - er, Je - sus is pur - er, He makes the sor-rowing
29
pp
p
spi - rit sing. Beau - ti - ful Sa - viour!
pp
p
33
Lord of the na - tions! Son of God and
37
Son of Man! Thee will I hon - our,
41
praise, and give glo - ry, Give praise and glo - ry ev - er -
45
pp
meno mosso
rit.
- more, give praise and glo - ry ev - er - more!
pp

Benediction

David Warner

MACK WILBERG

*The keyboard part may be played on piano or organ and adapted as necessary.

© 2011 Oxford University Press, Inc. Assigned to Oxford University Press 2010. This edition © 2013.

13
Be-calm our fears, And bless our sleep -
espress., sim.
17
S./A.
- ing.
TENORS
mp
T.
Come to us this day, A-wake our hearts,
21
T.
Re-new our minds, And bless our ris - -

25
S.
A.
mp
Come to us this hour, Re-store our hope,
T.
- ing.
B.
mp
Come to us this hour, Re-store our
29
Con-firm our faith, And bless our liv - -
hope, Con-firm our faith, our liv - -

33
mf
Come to us, we pray, Re-ceive our love,
mp
mp
- ing. Come, we pray, Re - ceive our
mf
mf
Come to us, we pray, Re-ceive our
mp
mp
- ing. Come, we pray, Re - ceive our
37
Be-hold our joy, And bless our prais - -
mp
love, Be - hold our joy, our prais - -
mf
love, Be-hold our joy, our prais - -
mp
love, Be - hold our joy, our prais - -

41
mf
- ing. A - - men, a - -
mf
- ing. A - - men, a - -
mf
- ing. A - - men, a - -
mf
- ing. A - - men, a - -
mf
45
mf
mp
- men, a - men, a - men, a - -
mf
mp
- men, a - men, a - men, a - -
mf
mp
- men, a - men, a - men, a - -
mf
mp
- men, a - men, a - men, a - -
mp

49
p
- men, a - - men, a - men,
p
- men, a - - men, a - men,
p
- men, a - - men, a - men,
p
- men, a - - men, a - men,
p
poco rit.
slower
53
(stagger breathing)
p
a - - - - - men.
(stagger breathing)
p
a - - - - - men.
(stagger breathing)
p
a - - - - - men.
(stagger breathing)
p
a - - - - - men.
poco rit.
slower
p

for the Mormon Tabernacle Choir and Orchestra at Temple Square

Brother James's Air

JAMES LEITH MACBETH BAIN (*c.*1840–1925)
arr. MACK WILBERG

Psalm 23 (adap.)

*The keyboard part may be played on piano or organ and adapted as necessary.

© 2010 Oxford University Press, Inc. Assigned to Oxford University Press 2010. This edition © 2013

13
SOPRANOS & ALTOS unis. p
S./A.
My
T./B.
lead-eth me, he lead-eth me The qui - et wa - ters by.
17
S./A.
soul he doth re - store a - gain, And me to walk doth make With -
p
21
- in the paths of bless-ed-ness, E'en for his own name's sake, With -
25
S./A.
- in the paths of bless-ed-ness, E'en for his own name's sake.
mp
T./B.
Yea,

29
p
Yea, though I pass, Yet will I fear no ill;
though I pass thro' sha-dowed vale, Yet will I fear no ill; For
mp
33
For thou art with, thy staff me com - fort still.
thou art with me, And thy rod and staff me com - fort still. Thy
37
Rod and staff, com-fort still, com - fort still.
rod and staff me com-fort still, me com - fort still.

41
mp
My ta - ble thou hast
div. p
45
fur - nish - ed In pre - sence of my foes; My
48
head thou dost with oil a - noint, And my cup o - ver -
51
div.
- flows. My head thou dost with oil a - noint, And my cup o - ver -
55
- flows.
mp

59
unis. mf
Good -
unis. mf
mf
63
- ness and mer - cy all my days Will sure - ly fol - low
mf
66
me; And in my Fa - ther's heart al - way My
69
dwell - ing place shall be. And in my heart for

72
ev - er - more Thy dwell - ing place shall be.
mp
And
mp
75
poco rit.
p
Thy place shall
in my heart for ev - er - more Thy dwell - ing place shall
poco rit.
p
79
a tempo
rit.
be.
be.
a tempo
rit.
mp
pp

I sing the mighty power of God
O little town of Bethlehem

Isaac Watts (1674–1748), altd
Phillips Brooks (1835–95)

Trad. English
arr. MACK WILBERG

I 8', 4', 1⅓'
II 8'
Pedal 16', 8'

Joyfully ♩ = *c.* 112

SOPRANO
ALTO

TENOR
BASS

Joyfully ♩ = *c.* 112

ORGAN

I

mf

II

mp

4

S./A.

SOPRANOS & ALTOS *unis.* *mp*

I sing the might - y pow'r of God that
O lit - tle town of Beth - le - hem, How

II

This piece may be sung using either set of lyrics.

© Oxford University Press, Inc. 2011. Assigned to Oxford University Press 2010. This edition © 2013

7
made the moun - tains rise, that spread the flow - ing
still we see thee lie! A - bove thy deep and
I
II
10
seas a - broad and built the loft - y skies. I
dream - less sleep The si - lent stars go by. Yet
I
13
sing the wis - dom that or - dained the sun to rule the
in thy dark streets shin - eth The ev - er - last - ing

16
day; the moon shines full at his com - mand, and
light; The hopes and fears of all the years Are
(I)
II
19
all the stars o - bey.
met in thee to - night.
I
23
TENORS & BASSES unis. mp
T./B.
I sing the good - ness of the Lord that
O morn - ing stars, to - ge - ther Pro -
II

26
filled the earth with food; he formed the crea - tures
- claim the ho - ly birth, And prai - ses sing to
I
II
29
SOPRANOS mp
with his word, and then pro - nounced them good. Lord,
God the King, And peace to men on earth; For
I
how thy won - ders are dis - played
Christ is born of Ma - ry,
32
S.
A.
mp
Thy won - ders are dis - played wher - e'er I turn my
is born of Ma - ry, And gath - ered all a -
mp
T.
B.
mp
Lord, are dis - played
of Ma - ry,

*When using the alternative text (O little town of Bethlehem), this note should be held for a crotchet/quarter note.

44
flow'r be - low but makes thy glo - ries known; and
Beth - le - hem, De - scend to us, we pray; Cast
47
clouds a - rise, and tem - pests blow, by or - der from thy
out our sin, and en - ter in, Be born in us to -
II
50
S.
A.
throne; while all that bor - rows life from thee is
- day. We hear the Christ - mas an - gels The
(T. & B. unis.)
T./B.
I

53
Ev - 'ry - where that
Come to us, a -
ev - er in thy care, ' and ev - 'ry - where that
great glad ti - dings tell: , O come to us, a -
we can be,
- bide with us,
56
we can be, thou, God, art pre - sent there.
- bide with us, Our Lord Em - ma - nu - el.
II
I
poco rit.
59
SOPRANOS & ALTOS unis. mp
S./A.
And
O

62
slightly slower
ev - 'ry - where that we can be, thou,
come to us, a - bide with us, Our
mp
65
rit.
tempo I
God, art pre - sent there.
Lord Em - ma - nu - el.
68

Commissioned by Dr Frederic G. Sanford, II,
for the Harrisburg Singers, Harrisburg, PA. (Susan Beckley, conductor) and the American Composers' Choral Festival
and in loving memory of Mary Jane Sharpless Sanford

King of glory, King of peace

George Herbert (1593–1633)

MACK WILBERG

© Oxford University 2013

9
and, that love may nev - er cease, I will move thee.
mf
13
T./B.
mf
T.
B.
Thou hast grant-ed my re-quest, thou hast heard
mp
17
me; thou didst note my work - ing breast,

20
thou hast spared me.
mf
23
mf
S.
A.
Where-fore with my ut - most art I will sing thee,
T.
B.
mf
mp
27
and the cream of all my heart I will bring

30
S./A. unis. mp
thee.
Though my sins a - gainst me cried,
mf
mp
34
S.
A.
thou didst clear me,
And a - lone, when
37
they re - plied, thou didst hear me.
mf

40
S.
A.
T.
B.
mf
Sev'n_ whole days, not one___ in sev'n,___
mf
mp
43
I___ will praise_ thee; in___ my heart, though not_ in heav'n,
47
I___ can raise___ thee.___
mf

50
mp
Small it is, in this poor sort, to en - rol thee;
mp
mp
54
E'en e - ter - ni - ty's too short to ex - tol
57
mf
f
thee, to thee, to
mf
f
mf

61
thee.
T./B.
mf
Sev'n_ whole days, not
f
mp
64
T.
B.
one___ in sev'n, in___ my heart, though not___ in heav'n,
67
mf
S.
A.
small_ it is, in this___ poor sort, E'en_____ e - ter - ni -
T.
B.

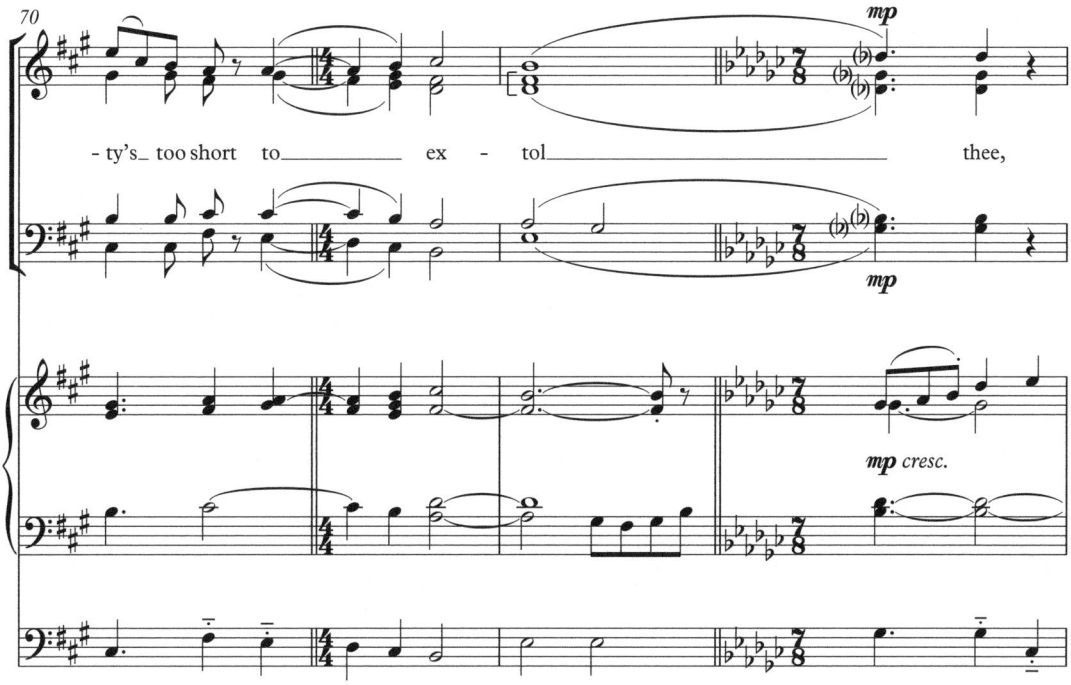
70
mp
- ty's_ too short to ex - tol thee,
mp
mp cresc.

74
mf
to thee, to thee.
mf
mf
f

78
ALTO
f
Sev'n_ whole days, not one_ in sev'n,
BASS
f
mf
81
S.
f
A.
in_ my heart, though not_ in heav'n, small_ it is, in
T.
B.
f
cresc.
84
this_ poor sort, e'en_ e - ter - ni - ty's_ too short, to_

87
ex - tol thee.
f
A -
f
Solo
(-Solo)
91
f
A - men!
- men!
cresc.
95
ff
A - men!
ff
ff

Morning has broken

Eleanor Farjeon (1881–1965)

Trad. Gaelic melody
arr. MACK WILBERG

Words: Eleanor Farjeon, from *Songs of Praise, Enlarged Edition*, Copyright © 1931, Oxford University Press. Renewed in USA 1959. Reprinted by permission of Harold Ober Associates.
Music: Copyright © 2008, Oxford University Press Inc. Assigned to Oxford University Press 2010. This edition © 2013.

Also available in a version for SATB and piano four-hands (ISBN 978-0-19-380463-0). Both this version and the orchestral accompaniment (see p. 4) have a more extended introduction to verses 1 and 2.

9
sing - ing, praise for the morn - ing, praise for them,
sweet - ness of the wet gar - den, spung in com -

11
1.
2.
spring - ing fresh from the Word!
- plete - ness where his feet pass.
mf (I.)
mp (II.)

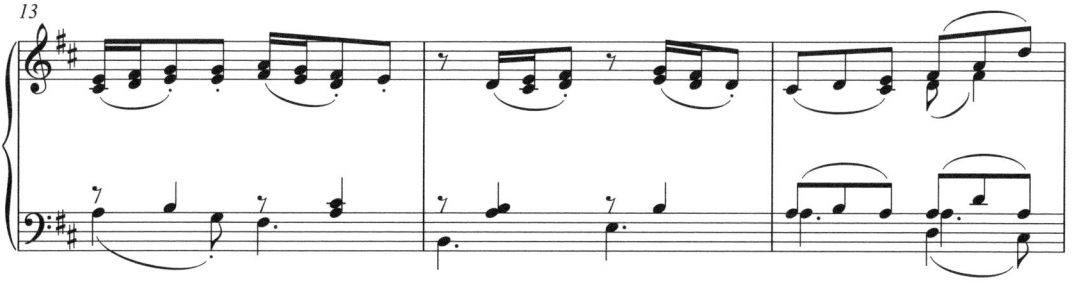
13

16
19
S.
A.
T.
B.
f
3. Mine is the sun - light; mine is the morn - ing, born of the
22
one light E-den saw play! Praise with e - la - tion, praise ev-'ry

25
morn - ing God's re - cre - a - tion of the new day!
28
dim.
30
SOPRANOS & ALTOS
unis. mp
S./A.
Praise with e - la - - tion, praise ev - 'ry
mp

32
rit.
morn - ing, God's re - cre - a - tion of the new
mp
35
a tempo
day!
mp
mp (Solo)
39
mp
II.

O Light of Life!

David Warner

MACK WILBERG

Copyright © 2008, Oxford University Press, Inc. Assigned to Oxford University Press 2010. This edition © 2013

15
hope when we fear, Deep - en our love— Thy Fire___ ap -
20
- pear! Light of our souls, Thou spark at our birth—
25
Grow bright in us, Shine in all the earth!
TENORS & BASSES
unis. mf
30
O Light of Life! O true Light of

35
Peace! Storms will a - rise, Let Thy light in - crease.
40
Pierce through dark clouds, Give pause to the proud; Let Thy shafts
45
fall, Lift hum - ble heads bowed. An - swer our pleas, Melt
50
hearts in Thy flame. Make us as one— As one in Thy

55
name.
mf
60
S.
A.
mf
O Light of Life! O
T.
B.
mf
65
sweet Life of Grace! Thou bidst us come, We fol - low a -

*Alternative lyrics.

84
clean, Send forth Thy white Dove. Fill us with
88
Fire, En - light - en our eyes; Help us to love— 'Tis
93
ff
price of the prize. Then let us come, En - robe us in
ff

98
white. Cleav - ing to Thee, Light un - to Thy

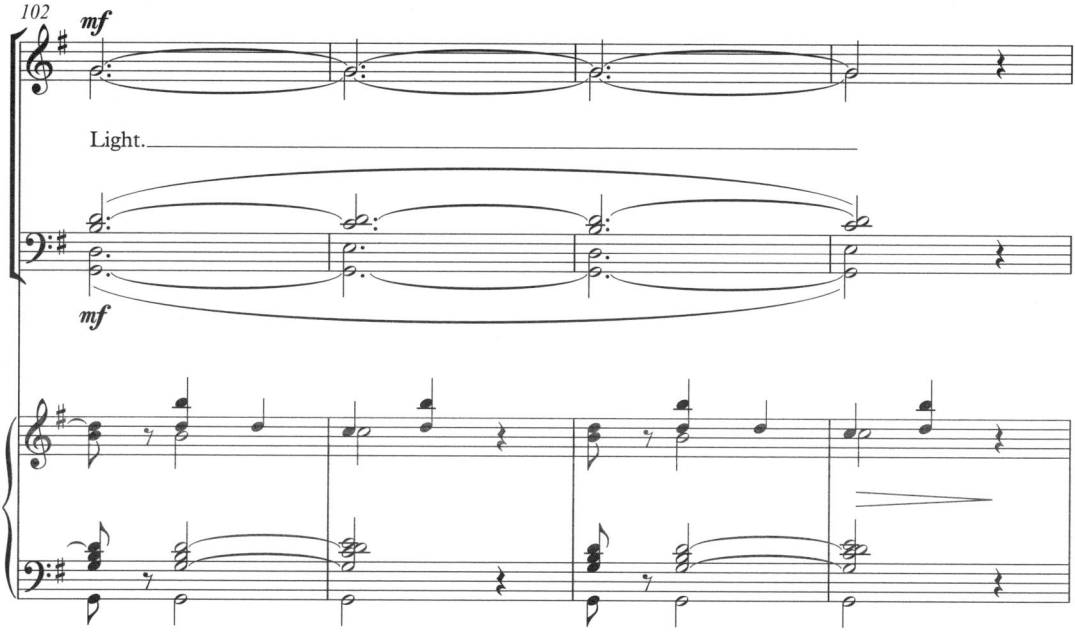
102
mf
Light.
mf

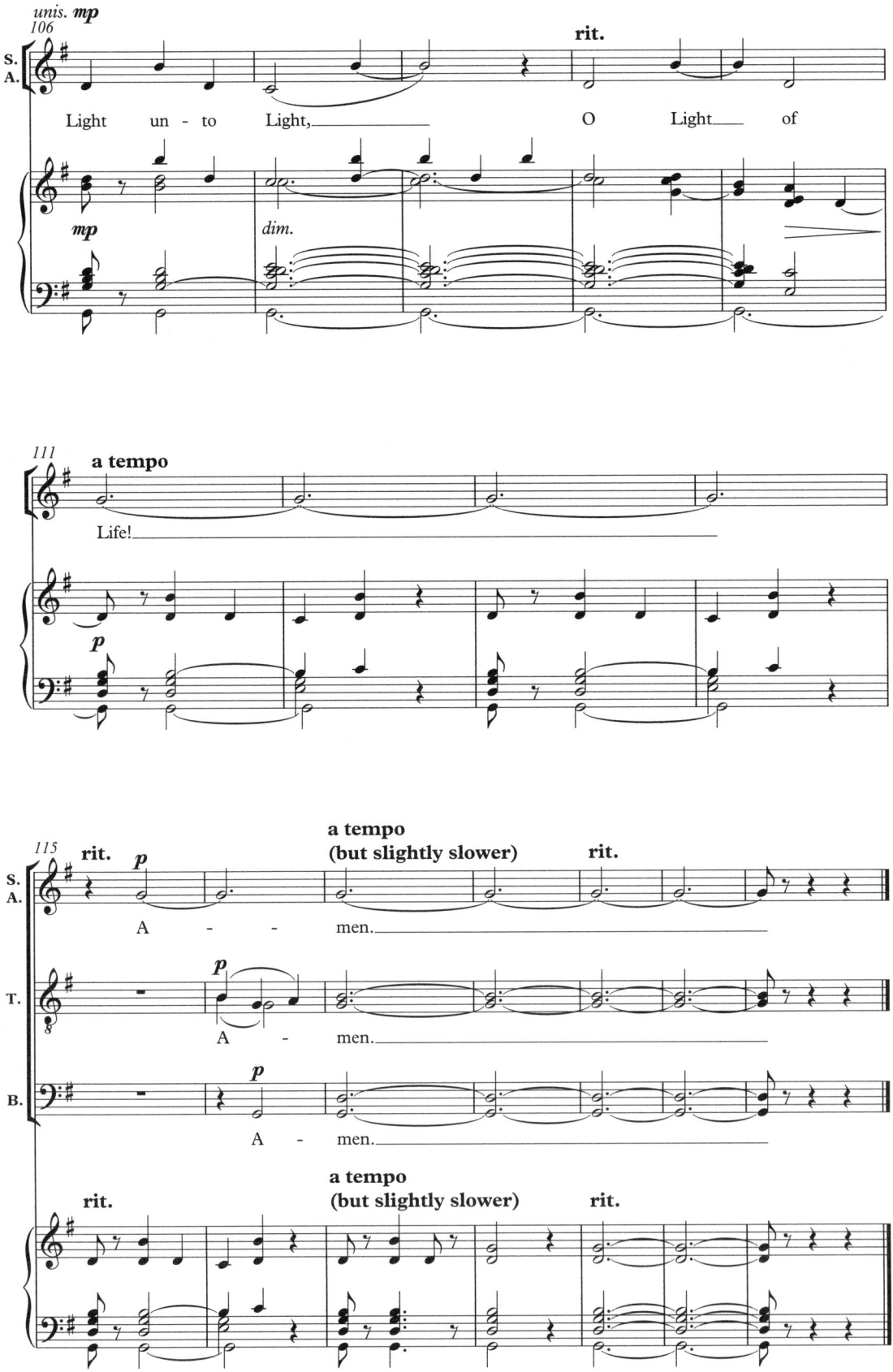
unis. mp
106
rit.
S.
A.
Light un - to Light, O Light of
mp
dim.
111
a tempo
Life!
p
115
rit.
p
a tempo
(but slightly slower)
rit.
A - men.
T.
p
A - men.
B.
p
A - men.
rit.
a tempo
(but slightly slower)
rit.

Commissioned in loving memory of Jack Richard Harding
for the Sanctuary Choir of Preston Hollow Presbyterian Church, Dallas, Texas; Terry Price, Director

O praise ye the Lord

Henry W. Baker (1821–77), alt.

C. HUBERT H. PARRY (1848–1918)
(Laudate Dominum)
arr. MACK WILBERG

© Oxford University Press 2013

13
ALL VOICES f unis.
O praise ye the
II
18
Lord! Sing praise in the height; Re - joice in his
(Ped.)
22
word, Ye an - gels of light; Ye heav - ens, a -

26
- dore him By whom ye were made, And wor - ship be -
30
- fore him, In bright - ness ar - rayed.
I
34

SOPRANO & ALTO
39
S.
A.
mf
O praise ye the Lord! Sing praise up - on
mf
II
43
earth, In tune - ful ac - cord, All ye of new
(Ped.)
47
birth; Praise him who hath brought you his grace from a -

51
- bove, Praise him who hath taught you to sing of his
I
55
love.
60
S.
A.
mf
O praise ye the
T.
B.
mf

64
Lord! All things that give sound; Each ju - bi - lant
68
chord re - e - cho a - round; Loud or - gans, his
p
(Ped.)
72
glo - ry forth tell in deep tone, And sweet harp, the
76
sto - ry of what he hath done.
mf
cresc.

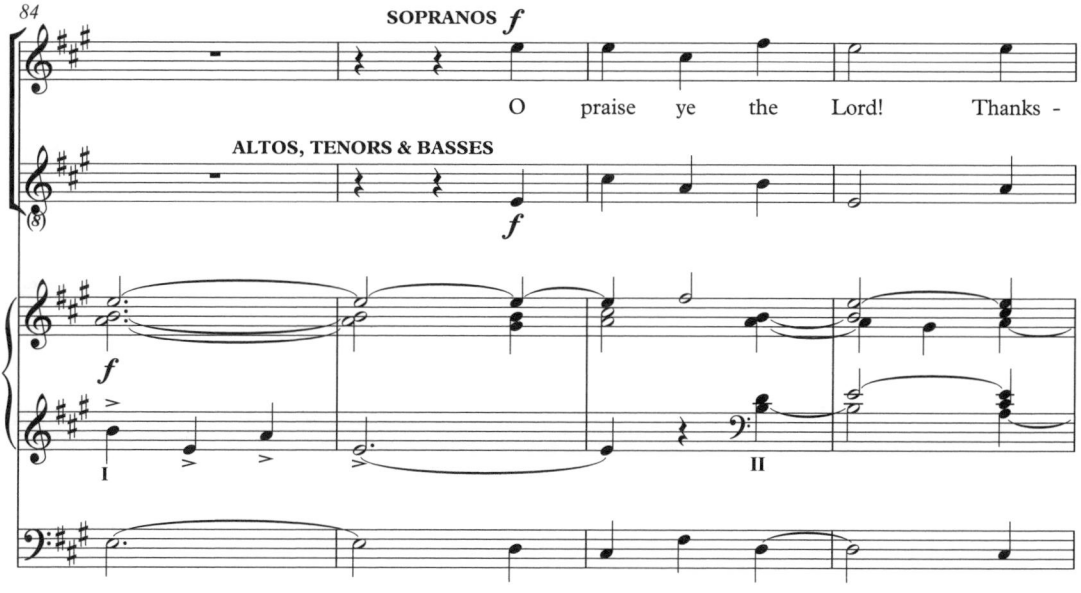
84
SOPRANOS f
O praise ye the Lord! Thanks -
ALTOS, TENORS & BASSES
f
f
I
II

88
-gi - ving and song To him be out - poured all

92
a - ges a - long! For love in cre - a - tion, for
96
hea - ven re - stored! For grace of sal - va - tion, O
100
praise ye the Lord!

104
S.
A.
T.
B.
ff
For grace of sal - va - tion, O praise ye
ff
II
108
the Lord. A - -
ff
I
112
rit.
- - - - men!
rit.
II

originally written for Brigham Young University Men's Chorus

The Morning Trumpet

John Leland (1754–1841)

B. F. White (1800–79)*
arr. MACK WILBERG

*From *The Sacred Harp* (1844).
**The 'h' of 'hear' should be given emphasis throughout.

© Oxford University Press

19
mount a-bove the skies When I hear the trum-pet sound in that morn -
24
- ing. O___ shout with glo - ry! I shall mount a-bove the skies When I
29
hear the trum - pet sound_ in that morn - - ing.
sound, sound the trum - pet, the trum - pet, the
33
unis.
But___ now I am a sol - dier, my cap-tain's gone be -
trum - pet, the trum - pet, the trum - pet, the trum - pet, the trum - pet, the
38
- fore, And I hear the trum-pet sound in that morn - ing. He's
trum - pet, the trum - pet, the trum - pet, the trum - pet, the trum - pet, the

43
giv - en me my or - ders and he bids me ne'er give o'er, Till I
trum - pet, the trum - pet, the trum - pet the trum - pet, the
47
f
hear the trum-pet sound in that morn - - ing. O___ shout with
trum - pet, the trum - pet, the trum - pet, the trump.
f
52
glo - ry! I shall mount a-bove the skies When I hear the trum-pet
56
sound in that morn - ing. O___ shout with glo - ry! I shall
61
mount a-bove the skies When I hear the trum - pet sound_ in that

65
mf
morn - - ing.
(Alto melody)
f
When
morn - ing, that morn - ing, that morn, in that morn.
mf
69
de - liv'd
shall I be de - liv - ered from this vain world of sin And shall
de - liv'd
73
morn, in that morn.
hear the trum - pet sound in that morn - - ing. And
morn, in that morn.
77
with my bless - ed Je - sus drink end - less plea - sures in, And shall
81
morn, in that morn.
hear the trum - pet sound in that morn - - ing. O
morn, in that morn.

85
f
shout with glo - ry! I shall mount a - bove the skies When I
f
89
hear the trum - pet sound in that morn - ing. O
93
shout with glo - ry! I shall mount a - bove the skies When I
97
mp cresc.
ff
morn - ing, in that
hear the trum-pet sound, sound in that morn, in that morn, in that
mp cresc.
ff
morn - ing, in that
morn - ing,
103
morn, in that morn, in that morn, in that morn, in that morn - ing.
morn - ing,